Our Earth

Kenneth Walsh

Consultant

Timothy Rasinski, Ph.D.
Kent State University

Publishing Credits

Dona Herweck Rice, *Editor-in-Chief*

Robin Erickson, *Production Director*

Lee Aucoin, *Creative Director*

Conni Medina, M.A.Ed., *Editorial Director*

Jamey Acosta, *Editor*

Stephanie Reid, *Photo Editor*

Rachelle Cracchiolo, M.S.Ed., *Publisher*

Image Credits

Cover narvikk/iStockphoto; p.4 Tong Chen/Dreamstime.com; p.5 top: Graeme Black/Shutterstock; p.5 bottom: Anat-oli/Shutterstock; p.7 rangizzz/Shutterstock; p.8 hddigital/Shutterstock; p.9 top: NASA/www.JSC Digital Image Collection; p.9 bottom: Sigapo/Shutterstock; p.10 Mark Schwettmann/Shutterstock; p.11 Volodymyr Goinyk/Shutterstock; p.12 Arand/iStockphoto; p.13 top: princessdlaf/iStockphoto; p.13 middle: Maresol/Shutterstock; p.13 bottom: Bill Kennedy/Shutterstock; p.14 Xaviarnau/iStockphoto; p.17 Orientaly/Shutterstock; p.18 Dmitriy Eremenkov/Shutterstock; p.19 Rick Nease-Illustrator/TFK; p.21 top: Kristijan Zontar/Shutterstock; p.21 bottom: crydo/Shutterstock; p.22 Bychkov Kirill Alexandrovich/Shutterstock; p.23 top Pecold/Shutterstock; p.23 bottom: oksix/Shutterstock; p.24 Elena Elisseeva/Shutterstock; p.25 top: Vera Kailova/Shutterstock; p.25 left: Andy Z./Shutterstock; p.25 right: akiyoko/Shutterstock; p.26 Computer Earth/Shutterstock; p.27 hironai/Shutterstock; p.28 YASAR/Shutterstock; back cover: Computer Earth/Shutterstock; background: s_oleg/Shutterstock; basketman23/Shutterstock

Based on writing from *TIME For Kids.*

TIME For Kids and the *TIME For Kids* logo are registered trademarks of TIME Inc. Used under license.

Teacher Created Materials

5301 Oceanus Drive
Huntington Beach, CA 92649-1030
http://www.tcmpub.com

ISBN 978-1-4333-3631-7

© 2012 Teacher Created Materials, Inc.

Table of Contents

A Big and Mighty Planet

Have you ever played in the dirt? Maybe it was warm and sandy and you let it sift through your fingers.

Maybe it was cool and muddy and you shaped it like clay.

Either way, you did something pretty amazing. You held one small part of a big and mighty **planet** in your hands. You held part of our planet, Earth.

The Big, Blue Marble

From Sun to Earth

How far is Earth from the sun? 92,897,000 miles!

Earth is part of our **solar system**. That means it is one of eight planets that **orbit** our sun. Earth is the third planet from the sun.

In Orbit

To orbit means to move in the path of a circle or oval around an object. Earth moves about 45,000 miles per hour!

Something orbits Earth, too. It is our moon.

People say that from the moon, Earth looks like a big, blue marble.

Water, Water Everywhere

Why does Earth look blue from space? The reason is there is much more water than land on Earth's surface.

Glaciers

A glacier is a large body of ice that spreads across an area of land or moves slowly down a hill or valley.

Water covers 70% of Earth's surface. Most of that water is in oceans. A small part is in lakes and rivers or frozen in **glaciers** and ice caps at Earth's north and south poles.

Water is important on Earth. Earth is the only planet in our solar system that holds living things, and every living thing needs water.

Life on Other Planets?

Other planets have water, but they do not have everything else that is needed for life, such as comfortable temperatures and good air to breathe.

Water also changes Earth. Large
amounts of water are very powerful.
Rivers and glaciers cut into Earth's
surface over time.

Water Fact

Earth's oceans are five times deeper than the average height of the land.

For example, the Colorado River slowly carved out the Grand Canyon over six million years!

Earth's Atmosphere

There is something else just as important as water on Earth. It is air.

Air makes up Earth's **atmosphere** (AT-muhs-feer). The atmosphere is like a big, thick blanket wrapped around Earth. The air we breathe from the atmosphere is called **oxygen** (OK-si-juhn). We breathe it as a gas. It has no taste, color, or smell. Oxygen is also part of water.

How Big?

Earth's atmosphere reaches for hundreds of miles away from Earth's surface.

Air

Air is made up of different kinds of gases. Nitrogen and oxygen make up most of the air in Earth's atmosphere.

The atmosphere is also important because it protects life on Earth. It absorbs energy from the sun, and it blocks the sun's harmful rays.

Earth's atmosphere is made of several layers. Weather takes place in the layer nearest Earth, which is about 10 miles high.

Layers of the Atmosphere

thermosphere

mesosphere

ozone layer

stratosphere

troposphere

Inside Earth

Earth is also made of several layers. The surface is called the **crust**. It is a cold, rocky layer about 60 miles deep. It is made of large pieces called **plates** that move and bump together, causing earthquakes, volcanoes, and other powerful activities.

Below the crust is the **mantle**. It is about 1,800 miles deep. It is made of hot, liquid rock and gas.

In Earth's center is the **core**. The core is more than 2,000 miles wide. The temperature there is so hot that it can reach as high as 12,000° F! How hot is that? The hottest day recorded on Earth's surface was just 136° F.

Earth Layers

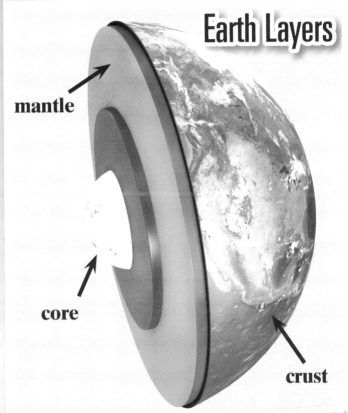

mantle

core

crust

layers of rock
in the crust

Earth History

Scientists believe that Earth is about 4.65 billion years old. At first, Earth was very hot and liquid. There was no life. Life came much later.

Earth's Size

Compared to other things in space, how big is Earth? Imagine this. If the sun were the size of a soccer ball, Earth would be the size of a sunflower seed—without the shell!

The shape of Earth formed over time, too. Slopes and valleys that exist today did not always exist. Water and wind have shaped some of them. Earth's movements have shaped others.

People have changed Earth, too. Roads, buildings, factories, and dams change Earth. Pollution changes it, too, but not for the better.

Ball or Egg?

Is Earth round like a ball? No! It is shaped more like an egg.

Living things on Earth have also changed over time. Long ago, dinosaurs roamed. There are no dinosaurs now, but scientists think that some birds may be related to them.

Plants and animals change over time. They change to become healthier and stronger.

Pteranodon
(flying dinosaur)
wingspan: 25 feet

California gull
(modern bird)
wingspan: 4 feet

Earth never stops changing. It is not the same today as it was when it began. Millions of years from now, it will not be the same as it is today.

Glossary

atmosphere—the layers of air surrounding and protecting Earth

core—the hot center layer of Earth

crust—the cold, rocky surface layer of Earth

glaciers—the large bodies of ice that move slowly over land

mantle—the middle layer of Earth made of hot, liquid rock and gas

orbit—to move in the path of a circle or oval around an object

oxygen—a colorless, tasteless, and odorless gas in Earth's atmosphere that people breathe

planet—a large body in space that orbits a star

plates—the moving sections of Earth's crust

solar system—a group of planets and other heavenly bodies that move around a central sun